How **good**
is our **school?**

Libraries
Supporting Learners

ISBN: 0-7053-1065-5

HM Inspectorate of Education
Denholm House
Almondvale Business Park
Almondvale Way
Livingston
EH54 6GA

Produced for HMIE by Astron B40295 5-05

Published by HMIE, May, 2005

Contents

	page
Introduction	1
How to use this guide	3
Glossary	9
Quality Indicators	10
Case Studies	20

Introduction

This document is one of a series of guides to self-evaluation. It builds on the advice given in *How good is our school?* (revised edition 2002) and, more specifically, *Taking a Closer Look at the School Library Resource Centre* published in 1999. This guidance is intended for use in the primary, special and secondary sectors.

School library resource centres support the development of successful learners and confident individuals. Promoting skills for lifelong learning encourages pupils to grow as responsible citizens who make an effective contribution to society. It is in the school library resource centre that all pupils have the opportunity to exercise their entitlement to access information and to develop comprehensive literacies in a supportive environment.

An effective school library resource centre is one which is central to the learning and teaching taking place in the school. Its vibrancy can help meet the needs of all learners, encourage imagination, independent study and self-directed learning. This empowers young people and encourages them to develop into lifelong learners. The specific contribution of the school library resource centre includes:

- access to a wide range of information;
- development of information literacy;
- effective use of ICT in learning and teaching; and
- promotion of reading for enjoyment.

Whereas there is some consistency between library resource centres in secondary schools, in primary and special schools they vary widely. Leadership, ongoing financial commitment, accommodation and staffing are key factors in the effectiveness of all school library resource centres. There are many examples of best practice where pupils are introduced to the joys of reading for pleasure, discover how to find and use information, and develop their abilities to learn independently and in groups.

The role of school librarians in the secondary sector cannot be underestimated. Their understanding of different learning styles and collaboration with teaching colleagues enables them to act as a bridge between young people, teachers, information and the curriculum. Their potential contribution towards meeting the National Priorities for Education is therefore considerable.

The professional and practical help offered from central school library support services will assist in the quality assurance process outlined in this document. Integrated community schools will also be involved in partnership working: with Careers Scotland, social work services, community learning and development, Dialogue Youth, public libraries, and with associated schools and pre-school centres.

The document and its case studies outline how quality indicators can be used by library staff and school managers to illustrate the impact of effective practice on learning and teaching and raising pupil attainment. This, in turn, will enable effective planning for improvement.

School Libraries and the National Priorities

1. Attainment and achievement	Libraries in schools play a crucial role in supporting pupils' attainment and achievement. They offer opportunities to motivate and raise the expectations and ambitions of learners. The distinctive environment of the school library resource centre can assist pupils in developing confidence in making choices and using their preferred learning styles.
2. Framework for learning	The school library resource centre can contribute to the ethos of the school and to positive behaviour. It can also provide support for teachers' professional development.
3. Equality and inclusion	All pupils, irrespective of ability, aspiration, economic or cultural background, benefit from an accessible school library resource centre with a broad range of resources. The active participation of pupils in improving the school library resource centre fosters a sense of ownership.
4. Values and citizenship	Active citizenship and lifelong learning depend on the ability to develop and use independent and transferable learning skills. Pupils' use of the school library resource centre supports their growing confidence in making choices, thinking independently and accepting responsibility as citizens.
5. Lifelong learning	Active teaching of generic learning skills helps pupils to develop into independent, lifelong learners. Programmes provide skills for life beyond school, encouraging critical thinking and positive attitudes to teamworking.

How to use this guide

This guide is designed to offer support and information to those with responsibilities relating to resource provision and the learning, information and cultural needs of pupils and staff in schools. The indicators and case studies provide a toolkit for managers, library and teaching staff to use in evaluating the quality and effectiveness of their school library resource centre.

The guide is structured in the following way:

The quality indicators

These pages offer a framework for evaluation with clear guidance on the key questions to ask and the reason why they are important. The indicators, which are presented in two sections, are those considered most relevant to evaluating the impact of the school library resource centre. The first section highlights three key indicators for the school senior management team. The section that follows presents seven key indicators for practitioners in the school library resource centre setting.

The case studies

Examples have been chosen from schools across Scotland and reflect best practice. They exemplify the key quality indicators in action and include the following features:

- co-operative approaches to identifying pupils' needs in planning, designing and delivering learning (including partnership work among library staff, teachers, classroom assistants, the senior management team and external agencies);

- differentiated experiences and resources to include pupils with additional support needs;

- transferable research models for use across the curriculum and year groups;

- creation of stimulating and exciting environments when designing or refurbishing school libraries;

- independent learning skills;

- pupil consultation as part of the continuous development of school library resource centres;

- positioning of the school library resource centre at the heart of literacy activities;

- development of information literacy resources and initiatives; and

- involvement of senior management teams and appropriate staff in the self-evaluation process.

Additional case studies are available on the web at www.slainte.org.uk. *Taking a Closer Look at the School Library Resource Centre* (1999) is also available at the same web address and contains Level 2 and Level 4 illustrations for a range of indicators. Enquiries concerning the case studies should be made to the Scottish Library and Information Council (SLIC) www.slainte.org.uk.

How are you going to find the evidence?

Many sources of evidence can be considered and compared in order to make an assessment of the contribution of the school library resource centre. Here are some examples:

Consult learners and staff

- Feedback, oral or written, from discussions with learners and staff about specific activities.
- Formal discussion with pupils, teachers and library staff in library committees, working groups and other members of the school community.
- Surveys, questionnaires.
- Feedback from wider school community, such as careers staff, School Board and parents.

Observe activities

- Examine the use of the school library resource centre and the range of resources available.
- Observe individual pupils using the facilities for a range of purposes.
- Watch and listen to pupils working together.
- Review the school library resource centre environment, including displays.

Analyse quantitative evidence

- Frequency of pupil and class interaction with library staff in relation to specific activities.
- Percentage of pupils participating in information skills activities (whole school and by stage).
- Percentage of pupils participating in extra-curricular reading activities (whole school and by stage).
- Percentage of pupils using the school library resource centre outwith timetabled class time (whole school and by stage).
- Trends over time in relation to these measures.
- Percentage of the school budget allocated to the library and increase/decrease over time.
- Frequency with which particular resources are borrowed.

Examine documentation and resources

- School library resource centre development plan

  – Monitoring and evaluation logs

  – Standards and quality reports

- Programmes and activities

  – Notes of planning meetings

  – Course materials

  – Forward plans of library/teaching staff

  – Action plans for library courses and programmes, plans for classwork

- Arrangements for library staff to receive curriculum information

- Evidence of library staff involvement in curriculum meetings

- Pupils' work in class and school library resource centre

  – Pupils' folders, log books and diaries

  – Pupils' records/profiles

  – Tasks and assignments

  – Pupils' self-assessments

  – Achievement awards lists

- School and library resource centre policies

- Range of resources in relation to a school's diverse population

- School and staff handbooks, school newsletters and local newspapers.

Gathering evidence

Note the sources of evidence on which
you are basing your evaluation.

Learners and staff consulted:

Observation activities undertaken:

Quantitative evidence:

Documentation and resources examined:

Other sources:

Fill in the strengths and areas for improvements for each of the
main key questions on the tables provided later in the document.

> **Consider your overall evaluation for each indicator and complete the following grid.**

Quality Indicators for school managers – to support and challenge	Overall evaluation
QI 2.1 Overall quality of attainment	
QI 6.5 Effectiveness and deployment of staff	
QI 7.3 Planning for improvement	
Quality Indicators for library staff – to develop and evaluate	**Overall evaluation**
QI 1.2 Courses and programmes	
QI 2.1 Overall quality of attainment	
QI 3.3 Pupils' learning experiences	
QI 3.4 Meeting pupils' needs	
QI 5.1 Climate and relationships	
QI 5.2 Expectations and promoting achievement	
QI 7.2 Self evaluation	

> **Review the areas for improvement which you have identified.**

> **Prioritise development areas.**

> **Identify criteria for success by which to judge progress. Include these in your development plan.**

Quality indicators are now based on six levels of performance.[1]

Level 6 Excellent

- Clearly excellent or outstanding.
- Very best practice worth disseminating beyond the school.
- Pupils' experiences and achievements are of a very high quality.
- Very high levels of performance which are sustainable.

Level 5 Very good (previously level 4)

- Major strengths.
- A high, but achievable standard of provision.
- The very few weaknesses, if there are any, do not diminish pupils' experience.
- Schools will take opportunities to improve and strive to raise performance to excellent.

The questions and case studies in this guide relate to the quality of provision or outcomes which would be evaluated as very good.

Level 4 Good

- Provision with important strengths that have a significant positive impact.
- Areas for improvement diminish the quality of pupils' experiences in some way.
- Schools will seek to improve further the areas of important strength while taking action to address areas for improvement.

Level 3 Adequate

- Provision where strengths just outweigh weaknesses.
- Pupils have access to a basic level of provision and strengths have a positive impact on pupils' experiences.
- Weaknesses do not have a substantially adverse impact, but do constrain the quality of pupils' experiences.
- Schools will seek to address areas of weakness while building on their strengths.

Level 2 Weak

- Weaknesses that are important enough to have a negative impact on the quality of pupils' experiences.
- Such weaknesses will be sufficient to diminish pupils' experiences in significant ways.
- There will be a need for the school to take structured and planned action to address weaknesses.

Level 1 Unsatisfactory

- Major weaknesses in provision.
- These weaknesses require immediate remedial action.
- Pupils' experience is at risk in significant respects.
- Improvement requires strategic action and support from senior managers.
- It may involve work alongside other staff and agencies in or beyond the school.

Glossary

Central Library Support Services – A central unit serving the whole local authority area and offering a range of resources and services to enhance the network of individual school library resource centres. These services are also known as Education Resource Services and School Library Services.

Library Staff – This term covers librarians, library assistants, learning assistants, classroom assistants or other support staff who have day-to-day responsibility for school library resource centre operation. It could also include parents or friends of the school who provide voluntary assistance.

Librarian – A person with a degree or a postgraduate diploma in librarianship and/or information science employed to work in a school library resource centre.

Out-of-class time – Time where pupils are not in formal, timetabled classes, e.g. lunchtime, breaks, before and after school.

Qualitative indicators – Tools for evaluating the value and effectiveness of services can be evaluated.

Quantitative indicators – A measure expressed in numerical terms. The unit of measurement will vary according to the context, e.g. money, time, percentage.

School Library Resource Centre – The library or resource area for staff and pupils in a school.

School Managers – Senior management team within primary, secondary and special schools.

Quality Indicators for school managers – to support and challenge

QI 2.1 Overall quality of attainment

This quality indicator is concerned with the following theme:

- *the school's progress in raising attainment*
- *pupils' progress in learning*
- *pupils' attainment in relation to national 5-16 levels and/or including examinations*
- *evaluations aims of the related quality indicators*

Questions to ask	Why is this important?	Evidence	
		Strengths	Areas for improvement
In what ways do you support and challenge staff with responsibility for the school library resource centre in order to ensure that it contributes to improvements in pupils' achievement and attainment?	The school library resource centre should support the learning needs of all pupils. It represents significant investment that must be accounted for in relation to impact on pupils' progress in learning. Library staff require leadership and guidance to make an effective contribution.		

Quality Indicators for school managers – to support and challenge

QI 6.5 Effectiveness and deployment of staff

This quality indicator is concerned with the following themes:

- *effectiveness of staff and teamwork*
- *deployment of staff*
- *provision for liaison to support pupils*

Questions to ask	Why is this important?	Evidence	
		Strengths	Areas for improvement
What active steps do you, as school managers, take to develop the effectiveness of library staff and support them in their work?	To be effective, policies and resources need to be in place to enable library staff to: • plan and work with teachers and other colleagues; • work with other resource providers, both local and national; • participate in Continuing Professional Development or appropriate training opportunities; • support the learning of teaching and support staff; and • support the work of pupils during and outwith school hours. School managers should have knowledge of the required competencies of library staff, and ensure these are developed to meet ongoing needs.		

Quality Indicators for school managers – to support and challenge

QI 7.3 Planning for improvement

This quality indicator is concerned with the following themes:

- *the development plan*
- *action planning*
- *the impact of planning*

Questions to ask	Why is this important?	Evidence	
		Strengths	Areas for improvement
As a manager, how do you ensure that the school development plan includes specific priorities relating to the school library resource centre?	It is the responsibility of managers to agree priorities and aims for the whole school, including the school library resource centre. In a secondary school the school library resource centre is treated like any other department in terms of its involvement in the development planning process in order that its improvement activities are systematically planned and completed.		
In what ways do you as managers monitor and evaluate progress made by the school library resource centre in meeting its targets?	Monitoring and evaluation of the school library resource centre by senior staff, in the context of national and local guidelines, ensures that prioritised targets are set and achieved as part of whole school improvement. The school library resource centre is included in reports on standards and quality as it makes an important contribution to the overall quality of education in the school.		

Quality Indicators for library staff – to develop and evaluate

QI 1.2 Courses and programmes

This quality indicator is concerned with the following themes:

- *breadth, balance and choice*
- *integration, continuity and progression*
- *support and guidance for staff*

Questions to ask	Why is this important?	Evidence	
		Strengths	**Areas for improvement**
In what ways does the school library resource centre contribute to breadth, balance and choice within courses and programmes across the school curriculum?	The prime function of the school library resource centre is to support its learning community. With its distinctively broad collection of resources supporting the development of information literacy, the school library resource centre is a major contributor to the range of learning experiences pupils can access in school.		
In what ways are school library resource centre activities integrated into a variety of courses and programmes in the school?	Productive links across the school ensure that the courses and programmes both offered and supported by the school library resource centre meet the range of needs, abilities and aspirations of learners. An overview of the curriculum helps to identify a variety of appropriate learning opportunities where this can be achieved. The senior management team, principal teachers, teachers, and library staff all have a role to play.		
To what extent do library staff receive comprehensive and helpful guidance and support on courses and programmes of work and their delivery?	Effective collaborative planning between teaching and library staff leads to the development of effective school library resource centre activities, the selection of appropriate resources and the production of differentiated support materials. Pupils' learning needs are best met when advance information about the developing curriculum is shared with library staff.		

Quality Indicators for library staff – to develop and evaluate

QI 2.1 Overall quality of attainment

This quality indicator is concerned with the following themes:

- *pupils' progress in learning*
- *pupils' attainment in relation to 5-14 and/or in national examinations*
- *evaluations across other related quality indicators*

Questions to ask	Why is this important?	Evidence	
		Strengths	Areas for improvement
How does the school library resource centre contribute to raising pupils' attainment and achievement?	The contribution of the school library resource centre to pupils' attainment and achievement is the key principle in its establishment. School libraries represent significant investment, which must be accounted for in terms of their impact on pupils' achievement and experiences.		
In what ways do pupils make progress in their learning in the school library resource centre?	The school library resource centre offers a widely differentiated range of learning experiences and resources, meeting a variety of learning styles. Pupils will have access to the school library resource centre, appropriate to their learning needs.		
To what extent are pupils able to use the school library resource centre themselves for research and recreation?	The ways in which pupils themselves use the school library resource centre, and when, will reflect the relevance of the school library resource centre to their perceived needs and to their developing abilities as independent lifelong learners.		

Quality Indicators for library staff – to develop and evaluate

QI 3.3 Pupils' learning experiences

This quality indicator is concerned with the following themes:

- *extent to which the learning environment stimulates and motivates pupils*
- *pace of learning*
- *personal responsibility for learning, independent thinking and active involvement in learning*
- *interaction with others*

Questions to ask	Why is this important?	Evidence	
		Strengths	Areas for improvement
How does the environment of the school library resource centre promote learning?	The design of a school library resource centre impacts directly on pupils' ability to learn. Pupils will be motivated by a creative environment and a range of resources which relate to their curricular, personal and cultural needs.		
To what extent do staff use information about pupils' learning to inform and plan their next steps in library-related learning?	A school library resource centre should contribute to a progressive approach to the acquisition of skills by pupils through partnership working between teaching, library, and support staff. An appropriate pace of learning, built on an awareness of individual needs, enables pupils to make good progress in their coursework. The continuing development of literacy, ICT and information skills will contribute to pupils' attainment.		
In what ways do pupils use the school library resource centre to learn independently?	Active citizenship and lifelong learning depend on the ability to develop independent and transferable learning skills. Successful learners are able to access and learn from a range of sources. The distinctive environment of the school library resource centre's facilities and resources can assist pupils in developing confidence in making choices, using their own learning styles, thinking independently and taking responsibility.		
Are there opportunities for pupils to interact with each other in library-related activities?	Best practice indicates that learning together is highly effective. The environment of the school library resource centre offers various opportunities for group work, which contribute to pupils' personal and social development.		

Quality Indicators for library staff – to develop and evaluate

QI 3.4 Meeting pupils' needs

This quality indicator is concerned with the following themes:

- *choice of tasks, activities and resources*
- *provision for pupils with differing abilities and aptitudes*
- *identification of learning needs*

Questions to ask	Why is this important?	Evidence	
		Strengths	Areas for improvement
To what extent does the range of tasks, activities and resources available in the school library resource centre make provision for the needs of all pupils?	The opportunity to make choices motivates learners, as does the recognition of prior achievement and individual social and cultural backgrounds. Children and young people need to feel that they matter. Their views should be sought when developing courses and matching resources to meet their individual needs.		
What evidence is there that tasks, activities and resources are matched to pupils' individual needs?	It is important to ensure that all pupils are challenged and supported at an appropriate level in order to reach their full potential. Differentiation is achieved by providing a range of resources, tasks or outcomes.		
In what ways is pupils' library-related learning supported by staff from different disciplines with a variety of expertise?	Good practice and the principles of integrated community schools advocate that staff from a range of disciplines work together for the benefit of learners. Through these partnerships, barriers to learning can be diminished.		
What contributions do the school library resource centre and the library staff make to supporting pupils in achieving their personal goals and in pursuing their individual interests?	Active teaching of generic learning skills helps pupils to develop into independent, lifelong learners. Involving pupils in the continuous development of the school library resource centre will ensure its relevance to their needs.		

Quality Indicators for library staff – to develop and evaluate

QI 5.1 Climate and relationships

This quality indicator is concerned with the following themes:

- *sense of identity and pride in the school*
- *reception and atmosphere*
- *pupil and staff morale*
- *pupil/staff relationships*
- *pupils' behaviour and discipline*

Questions to ask	Why is this important?	Evidence	
		Strengths	Areas for improvement
What evidence is there that pupils value the school library resource centre and are engaged in making decisions about its development?	Consulting with pupils on school library resource centre developments encourages a sense of ownership, leads to active use of the school library resource centre and contributes to a positive school ethos.		
To what extent does the school library resource centre provide a welcoming and inclusive environment, reflecting the values of the school and its community as a whole?	The school library resource centre makes a significant contribution to the school and its community by being a welcoming, attractive and safe environment.		
In what ways does the school library resource centre promote issues of inclusion and equality across the school community?	Everybody should have access to the school library resource centre as a whole school resource. Library staff and the school library resource centre have key roles in promoting positive attitudes towards equality and diversity, leading to an inclusive ethos and good pupil-staff relationships.		
To what extent does the school library resource centre promote and uphold the positive behaviour policy of the school? What evidence is there of its success?	The school library resource centre needs to implement school policies actively and consistently to contribute to high standards of pupil behaviour and discipline, and to stimulate a concern and understanding for others.		

Quality Indicators for library staff – to develop and evaluate

QI 5.2 Expectations and promoting achievement

This quality indicator is concerned with the following themes:

- *pupil and staff expectations and use of praise*
- *promoting an ethos of achievement*

Questions to ask	Why is this important?	Evidence	
		Strengths	Areas for improvement
In what ways does the school library resource centre communicate and reinforce high expectations of pupils in the work they are undertaking there?	The school library resource centre should play its part in supporting pupils to achieve their full potential. When staff plan together, they share their expectations for pupils' achievement.		
What evidence is there that the library-related achievements of pupils are recognised and celebrated by the school?	It is important for pupils that their work in the school library resource centre be evaluated and valued. This will build confidence and self-esteem. It will also reinforce the school library resource centre as a valid and productive learning environment.		
How do library staff communicate the value of transferable learning skills, and the role of these skills, in raising pupil achievement?	To develop as independent and aspirational learners throughout school and in life, pupils need to be taught learning skills overtly. Pupils need to be helped to recognise the importance of these generic skills in achieving success in school and the wider world.		

Quality Indicators for library staff – to develop and evaluate

QI 7.2 Self evaluation

This quality indicator is concerned with the following themes:

- *processes of self-evaluation*
- *monitoring and evaluation*
- *reporting on standards and quality*

Questions to ask	Why is this important?	Evidence	
		Strengths	Areas for improvement
What evidence is there that the self-evaluation carried out in relation to the school library resource centre has resulted in measurable and observable improvements in the quality of the service and a positive impact on pupils' achievements and experiences?	Without self-evaluation it is not possible to develop a high-quality service which meets the needs of users. A collaborative approach and the involvement of the whole school community ensure the activities reflect the curriculum being delivered in the school. The self-evaluation process will lead to the identification of strengths, development needs and planning priorities.		
What long-term targets for continuous improvement have been identified as a result of ongoing monitoring and evaluation?	Monitoring and evaluation of the school library resource centre by library staff and senior staff will help to ensure that prioritised agreed targets are set and achieved, within the improvement cycle.		
How well integrated are the school library resource centre's development planning processes and its approaches to reporting on standards and quality within the school's quality processes?	The senior management team, school staff and authority staff require robust information about the ongoing developments and progress of the school library resource centre to inform whole school planning.		

Case Study 2.1 For Managers

QI 2.1 Overall quality of attainment

This case study is concerned with the following theme of the quality indicator:

- *pupils' progress in learning*

The school is a rural high school with 400 pupils. The school library resource centre has one full-time member of staff and one part-time member of staff who has been allocated additional hours to support the three associated primary schools.

The library staff have been working to add value to the classroom teaching in specific areas of the curriculum, through poetry, creative writing and developing a reading habit. Pupils in P4-P7 have been developing a range of language skills and confidence.

Specific initiatives include:

- creative writing emphasising the use of characterisation to tell a story;

- using National Tell a Story Day as a catalyst for creative writing; introducing onomatopoeia and alliteration in writing poetry; and

- poetry writing linked to emotions; and extending the reading habit through enabling access for P7 pupils to the wider range of resources of the secondary school library.

By providing services to the staff and pupils, the library staff have the opportunity to engage in a variety of delivery techniques, such as:

- visiting a local cemetery to initiate story writing;

- providing extensive book resources to encourage reading with the added value of staff supporting pupils as they learn to select books of their choice;

- engaging in poetry workshop with pupils; and

- building partnerships with outside agencies like the local theatre for story telling.

The work of the library staff has added value to the classroom work and pupils are reading more widely. There is increased confidence in making choices, which is motivating pupils to use resources. Through use of the Accelerated Reading programme pupils are tested on their knowledge and understanding of books they have read, thus tracking their progression from P7 to S1. The quality and range of poetry reading has been extended.

Key features of success

- The quality of the pupils' work has improved.

- Creativity and literacy have been encouraged.

- Pupils have demonstrated their ability to write creatively from a range of sources and experiences.

- Pupils grew in confidence in making their own reading choices.

- Pupils were encouraged to read for enjoyment.

- Partnership working involved commitment from staff within the school and external agencies.

Case Study 6.5 – For Managers

QI 6.5 Effectiveness and deployment of staff

This quality indicator is concerned with the following themes:

- *effectiveness of staff and teamwork*

- *deployment of staff*

- *provision for liaison to support pupils*

This primary school is in a village on the outskirts of a large town, and has a roll of 302 and a nursery with 30 children attending in the morning and 30 in the afternoon. The school library resource centre was refurbished in 2000. Responsibility for the school library resource centre falls within the remit of the head teacher. Policies and guidelines are in place for the management of the library and the responsibilities of staff and pupils in its use.

The library is well used on a regular timetabled basis, with every class from the nursery to P7 using their time allocation to change books, read and carry out research linked to topic work, and use the interactive whiteboard with a variety of software applications.

The library books are in good condition and are very well used. This is due to the effective supervision of library use by class teachers, school support staff and parent helpers. The crossing patrol assistant runs the library, spending time in it three days a week, to keep the ALICE computerised library management system running smoothly and to work with the four parent helpers who regularly spend time tidying the library. The head teacher has encouraged some of these parents to apply for support staff posts within the school. This has been to the benefit of the school and to the individuals by promoting the take up of local employment. Four pupils act as library prefects, taking responsibility for tidying the library at the end of every day with the helper. Their photographs are displayed in the library, recognising their active involvement.

The display in the library on 'What's your favourite book?' is very imaginative and effective, promoting reading development. Two members of the support staff have received training provided by the authority and this has been put to good use throughout the school, as well as in the library, in mounting displays of a high standard.

A range of reading promotion and story telling activities is supported. There is an annual book fair, with some of the money raised being used to buy new books for the library. Other events include a sponsored event for Readathon, and author visits. There are effective links with the council's library services. Pupils regularly contribute book reviews for publication in the library service's reading guide for young people.

Key features of success

- A range of staff and parent helpers.

- Pupils actively participating in the running of the library.

- The policy framework providing clear guidance to staff.

- Appropriate training opportunities are being given to staff.

- Effective partnerships with the Library Service continuing to develop.

- Pupils being encouraged to read for enjoyment.

Case Study 7.3 – For Managers

QI 7.3 Planning for improvement

This quality indicator is concerned with the following themes:

- *the development plan*

- *action planning*

- *the impact of planning*

This Primary School is in an urban setting, with a roll of 420 pupils across 15 classes. The school library resource centre has been newly remodelled.

The previous school library resource centre had become an abandoned area at the back of the school stage and it was recognised that it needed attention especially to support the reading for information component of the curriculum. Its redevelopment became a priority in the school development plan.

A school library resource centre development plan was compiled which considered:

- the physical environment; and

- the learning environment.

This involved:

- the inclusion of this task in the remit of a senior member of staff;

- the allocation of staff time;

- the allocation of money;

- the development of co-operative strategies with the Parent Teacher Association and support agencies, e.g. Education Resource Service (ERS); and

- specific fund-raising events such as a book fair.

The physical environment changed with the move of the school library resource centre away from the stage area to a dedicated room, with new furniture and furnishings. With the aid of the ERS the book stock was edited and enhanced to suit learners' needs.

Emphasis on the school library resource centre as a learning environment was developed through the establishment of 3 working parties representing the lower, middle and upper stages in the school. Among them they developed a 'Learning Path' for pupils from P1 to P7 in which *reading for information* was practised in the context of the curriculum which increased in complexity as skills were developed.

As classes undertake the 'Learning Path' they are timetabled to use the school library resource centre and have support from classroom assistants. It has only been operating for a few months. In this first stage monitoring and evaluation came from feedback from forward plans, face-to-face discussions with teaching staff and classroom assistants and written evidence in pupils' work. Further monitoring is planned for next session.

All pupils are now included in a planned approach to reading for information in the context of the curriculum. This ensures that skills are developed and reinforced over a period of time, with the impact on learning and attainment the key objective.

The acting headteacher has shared this experience within his learning community[1] including with the librarian at the secondary school. Discussion is taking place as to its extension to other schools in the cluster.

Key features of success

- Integration of the school library resource centre with the curriculum (both *reading for information* and topic work) and impact on learning.

- Involvement and commitment of all staff within the school, including classroom assistants, and external agencies.

- Pupil consultation as part of the continuous development of school library resource centres.

- Creation of a conducive learning environment with attractive surroundings and appropriate resources.

- Sharing information within the learning community.

[1] Integrated Community School

Case Study 1.2

QI 1.2 Courses and programmes

This quality indicator is concerned with the following themes:

- *breadth, balance and choice*

- *integration, continuity and progression*

- *support and guidance for staff*

The comprehensive secondary school has a small roll, under 400 and is in a rural setting. Although the area does not have a deprivation status approximately one third of pupils qualify for free school meals. The school library resource centre has recently been refurbished and has a stock of around 6000 books and 18 computers, together with good study space. The library is run by a chartered librarian.

The librarian and social subjects department worked together to improve the project and information literacy skills of pupils through a topic on climatic regions for S1 pupils. The PLUS model[2] is a widely-used information skills model which uses the acronym PLUS as an easy way for pupils and teachers to break information skills into four main parts.

		The PLUS Model
P	Purpose	Identifying the purpose of an investigation or assignment
L	Location	Finding relevant information sources related to the purpose
U	Use	Selecting and rejecting information and ideas, reading for information, note-taking and presentation
S	Self-evaluation	How pupils evaluate their performance in applying information skills to the assignment and what they learn for the future

The PLUS model was integrated into library-based and classroom-based lessons on the biomes topic. The library-based lessons included sessions on planning, locating resources in the school library resource centre or on the internet, evaluating resources, note-taking and self evaluation.

---

[2] Herring, J (2004): The internet and information skills: a guide for teachers and school librarians. Facet Publishing.
Herring, J E, Tarter, A-M and Naylor, S (2002): An evaluation of the PLUS model to develop pupils' information skills in a secondary school. School Libraries Worldwide 8(1) January. 1-24

A full evaluation of the programme is to be carried out on completion. Based on the outcomes, a linked development for the same pupils in S2 will seek to revisit the skills learnt in their next social subjects project. The Science Department have adopted the same method for their S1 science topic. These developments link with other collaborative activity between the librarian and the Social Subjects Departments for S2 and S3 pupils. Pupils carry out library-based webquests and other work in the library on a wide range of topics.

Key features of success

- Pupils learn a method of research which aims to improve their work and which can be transferred across the curriculum and progresses from year to year.

- The consistent approach taken towards information literacy between departments benefits pupils and staff.

- The evaluation process has been developed to demonstrate success in attainment and independent learning skills.

- The quality of the pupils' work has improved.

- Pupils acquire lifelong learning skills in the search for, and evaluation of, different types of resources.

Case Study 3.3(1)

QI 3.3 Pupils' learning experiences

This quality indicator is concerned with the following themes:

- *extent to which the learning environment stimulates and motivates pupils*

- *pace of learning*

- *personal responsibility for learning, independent thinking and active involvement in learning*

- *interaction with others*

This is a large, urban school with 1200 pupils. The school library resource centre is in a 1980's extension, staffed by a chartered librarian and one classroom assistant (6 hours per week). The computer area has 7 desktop computers and 3 laptop computers.

The librarian has been leading an initiative which exchanges poetry and information between schools in two local authority areas in Scotland, and schools in Norway and the USA. Participation in the initiative is an option for English department staff but can be adapted into other curricular areas and is suitable for pupils of all abilities.

Pupils, the librarian, the classroom assistant, teachers and pupils/staff in the other schools are involved in an exchange of ideas and work between pupils, which aims to raise motivation by offering contact with groups outside the pupils' own school. Pupils are presented with a theme, such as their favourite author or a poem about their country, and are asked to write a piece a work. Links have been established between school librarians who facilitate the exchange through email. They manage the scheme and introduce work to pupils, who create word-processed documents using library resources to stimulate ideas. Librarians then exchange the poetry and information by email. Teachers promote the scheme in the classroom and monitor the quality of the work, whilst the classroom assistant displays the materials from the home school and other partners.

As a result of the programme pupils have a greater appreciation of their own work. Further exchanges are planned between the partners linked to events such as annual Robert Burns celebrations and the USA's national poetry month in April.

Key features of success

- Pupils know their work is viewed by the young people in other schools and are motivated by this.

- Pupils' work is displayed in the school library resource centre which allows it to be viewed by other classes, teachers and parents.

- Creativity and literacy are encouraged.

- ICT skills are applied in practice and for a real purpose.

- The project contributes to the school's activities in the field of International Education.

Case Study 3.3(2)

QI 3.3 Pupils' learning experiences

This quality indicator is concerned with the following themes:

- *extent to which the learning environment stimulates and motivates pupils*

- *pace of learning*

- *personal responsibility for learning, independent thinking and active involvement in learning*

- *interaction with others*

The school is in an urban setting with over 800 pupils on the school roll. The percentage of pupils entitled to free school meals is above the national average and pupils' attendance is well below the national average. The role of the librarian in promoting the use of the library and in developing pupils' skills in information and communications technology (ICT) is one of the key strengths of the school.

The need to teach pupils how to become independent learners had been identified and plans were made to support this through specific provision within curricular activities. The importance of the library in developing lifelong independent learners has been clearly recognised by the school and education authority.

Pupils are introduced to the library during initial P7 visits and timetabled to work in the library during that visit. The information skills which pupils had acquired at primary school are individually assessed by the librarian to ensure continuity and progression in learning.

S1 pupils are timetabled for a 6-8 week library skills course, with each class attending one period a week. The information handling skills and ethos developed through this course are reinforced, expanded and developed through co-operative working between subject departments and the school library resource centre as pupils progress through the school. For example, following the information skills course, pupils in S1 science use the skills learned in a library/science project on Energy. This expands and builds on the pupils' information skills course and allows them to use print, audio, visual, and electronic information sources to complete their research on energy.

All pupils have access to library resources in a curricular setting at all stages throughout the school. Pupils studying modern languages in S3 use library resources, with guidance and instruction, to carry out research on languages and countries. They present their finished work as a web page, which is added to the school's Intranet. The creation of the web page often involves many hours of pupils' leisure time with some of them making extensive use of the library before school and during lunch to finish their work. Pupils are given the opportunity to work independently at all stages with appropriate support.

Senior pupils use the library to investigate issues and topics and continue to improve their information handling skills. In Religious Education, for example, pupils are encouraged to choose how they present their finished research. Instructions and guidance are given on a variety of presentation options such as PowerPoint.

Co-operative working between subject departments and the school library resource centre builds a range of individual learning skills and pupils are encouraged to become confident independent learners. The pupils' use of the school library resource centre supports their growing confidence in making choices, thinking independently and taking responsibility for their learning.

Key features of success

- The central role of the library as a support for encouraging independent learners is recognised and valued.

- Pupils demonstrate their ability to access and learn from a range of sources.

- Independent and transferable learning skills are developed.

- Pupils' self-confidence and self-esteem are improved through the development of presentation skills, research skills and participation in group work.

Case Study 3.4

QI 3.4 Meeting pupils' needs

This quality indicator is concerned with the following themes:

- *identification of learning needs*

- *provision for pupils with differing abilities and aptitudes*

- *choice of tasks, activities and resources*

The school is situated in a housing scheme in a Social Inclusion Partnership area and has a roll of over 700 pupils. Over 10% of the pupils are children of asylum seekers, with English as an Additional Language (EAL). In 2002, along with the rest of the school the school library resource centre moved into newly built premises. It is run by a chartered librarian and contains a suite of over 20 networked computers, as well as books and multi-media resources.

The school was concerned about the information literacy needs of pupils without computers at home. Pupils with EAL were identified through liaison between the school librarian and support for learning teachers.

A programme of After School Supported Study was jointly planned by the school librarian, teaching staff from Support for Learning, EAL, English and Science departments and Senior Management Team members. Various components were identified that would encourage the development of information literacy skills:

ICT:

- word processing

- internet searching

- using email

Research skills:

- activities were carried out in English and Science classes using the theme of 'Animals'.

Reading skills:

- awareness-raising of features of English language such as idioms

- use of activities from a published 'reading game'.

Pupils with EAL were able to gain enhanced access to ICT facilities, learn and practise word processing and research skills and develop higher order reading skills. From this programme, their access to the mainstream curriculum was accelerated as they gained confidence in using ICT to support their studies and became increasingly familiar with English language idioms.

Key features of success

- The school has a co-operative approach to all aspects from identifying needs to planning, designing and delivering the programme.

- Support from the senior management team provides the allocation of essential resource support.

- The differentiated programme includes all pupils.

Case Study 5.2

QI 5.2 Expectations and promoting achievement

This quality indicator is concerned with the following themes:

- *pupil and staff expectations and use of praise*

- *promoting an ethos of achievement*

The school is an urban residential/day school for severely autistic pupils aged 5-18. Without easy access to a public library it is important that pupils had access to a school library. They require access to a wide range of materials which will encourage reading yet fulfil the needs of autistic young people. This means no ambiguity or fantasy, straightforward language, highly visual presentation, and appropriateness for age and development. The library is managed by a team of school staff.

Until recently the school library contained a varied collection of reading materials, acquired and arranged without a planned, pupil-centred approach. This reflected a lack of expectation that young people could make choices about their reading for enjoyment. Pupils had no involvement in, or responsibility for, the library and its development.

The senior management team (SMT) had identified that pupils had little opportunity to read for enjoyment. The development of the library featured in the school improvement plan. Education Resource Service staff provided support and together with the senior management team they identified the following problems:

- residential pupils did not have access to books to share with their carers;

- day pupils had few opportunities to access public libraries;

- the materials in stock did not appeal to pupils for a variety of reasons; and

- the display, arrangement and storage of the materials did not facilitate easy access.

A successful application was made for a Scottish Executive Home Reading Initiative Start-up Grant. This was supplemented by school funds.

Teachers and Education Resource Service staff developed criteria for selecting material for severely autistic pupils. The existing material was edited against the criteria. The library was reorganised using a labelling scheme that utilised the signs already used in school for non-verbal communication.

Staff and pupils discussed the materials which pupils would like in their library. As far as possible these suggestions were included during selection. Senior pupils met with Education Resource Service staff to discuss the type of library furniture required. Pupils are now more involved in the running of the library as a result of this initiative. This provides opportunities for them to be involved with other pupils and to take responsibility.

Staff are monitoring the impact of the school library by assessing its continuing popularity amongst pupils, the records of materials borrowed for out-of-school hours reading, and the continuing involvement of pupils in its management.

Key features of success

- An attractive library has been established which has the support and active involvement of pupils.

- The visual communication scheme is used consistently throughout the school.

- Young people can read or look at books for pleasure or information in an informal environment.

- Staff expectations have increased in relation to the way in which the library can be used to support learning.

- There is now an expectation amongst staff that pupils will comment on the choice of materials.

- Pupils have increased opportunity to work together co-operatively and to take responsibility for the development of the library.

Case Study 7.2(1)

QI 7.2 Self-evaluation

This quality indicator is concerned with the following themes:

- *processes of self-evaluation*

- *monitoring and self-evaluation*

- *reporting on standards and quality*

The school has a roll of 980, and serves pupils from a large urban conurbation. Ethos is a major strength of the school and the school has good arrangements for quality assurance. It had achieved external recognition of quality standards through Charter Mark and COSLA quality awards. The school library resource centre is attractive and well furnished and is staffed by a full time librarian. The librarian uses a three-step framework of planning and review – a *broad view*, a development plan and a standards and quality report.

In preparation for the quality assurance and planning process, the school librarian completes a *broad view* at the same time each year, before the school library resource centre plan or school development plan is produced. This is helpful in focusing on school library resource centre developments over the year and giving the school librarian and school management a general overview. It is an important preparatory part of the planning and review process, helping to identify priorities for the forthcoming year in correlation with and progression from those of previous years. The broad view illustrates strengths and points for action for the next school library resource centre development plan.

The development plan gives the librarian clear, achievable aims and a functional guide. By identifying priorities, resource needs and timetabling requirements can be assessed for the following year. The information provided by the broad view and development plan form the basis of the school library resource centre's standards and quality report each year.

The standards and quality report includes:

- an evaluation of selected quality indicators;

- key achievements;

- progress with the development plan;

- targets for the coming year;

- quantitative performance statistics; and

- a breakdown of the budget allocation.

Key features of success

- A report is produced giving the senior management team information on how the school library resource centre is progressing and highlighting key strengths of the service.

- By using the quality framework a consistent approach to self-evaluation is employed across the school.

- The school management team has more information about the contribution of the school library resource centre.

Case Study 7.2(2)

QI 7.2 Self-evaluation

This quality indicator is concerned with the following themes:

- *processes of self-evaluation*

- *monitoring and self-evaluation*

- *reporting on standards and quality*

The school has a roll of 900, and is located in a city suburb. The school was refurbished in 1996. Accommodation is generally good and the overall school ethos of inclusion and the morale of pupils and staff were identified as key strengths in a recent HMIE inspection. The school library resource centre is attractive and well furnished. It is relatively well sited in the community wing. It is staffed by a full-time librarian and a part-time library assistant.

Following her appointment, the librarian recognised that, whilst the school library resource centre was well regarded and had excellent accommodation, its impact on learning and teaching could be improved. After discussions with departments and the Head of School Library Service, she used the quality indicators to assess the current service, identify areas for improvement and plan future developments. She reported her findings to the headteacher and principal teachers of English and Environmental Studies. She identified what was needed to improve the pupils' learning in the school library resource centre.

One of her observations was to identify that while pupils were clear about what was expected of them in the school library resource centre, there was little evidence of the development of pupils' information and enquiry skills. Other weaknesses were also apparent. She could see little evidence of success in individual research; and knowledge of information sources and search strategies did not meet her expectations.

The development of an Information Skills course for S1 pupils was one of the many improvements she identified to meet this need, as well as improving teaching staff's awareness of the school library resource centre. Again, observations identified that whilst extensive independent use was made of the school library resource centre outside class time, there was little evidence of reading for enjoyment across the school. The action plan shows the development of strategies from promoting reading for enjoyment across the school, including reading lists for pupils of all ages, trips to reading events, book fairs and events to support World Book Day. Working with the Parent Staff Association, the school raised funds to improve the quality of the titles for younger pupils, and reading was encouraged by removing older stock and replacing it with modern and attractive resources.

At its inspection in 2003, the school library resource centre was highlighted as being a model for self-evaluation. The report recognised that the school librarian could play a role in assisting teachers to develop self-evaluation across the school. The school librarian's Library Resource Centre Profile, which was completed in preparation for the inspection, and her grid detailing the quality indicators, observations and actions clearly demonstrate ways in which self-evaluation can be used to lead to improvements in standards and quality.

Key features of success

- HMIE identified the school library resource centre as an area of excellence.

- The school librarian had identified areas for improvement and ways in which to develop.

- She had comprehensively self-evaluated and used this process to reflect on current practice and to help her future planning.

- Emerging and linked developments had been identified.

- Procedures for monitoring and evaluating the library were effective and informed planning.

- Plans to develop Information Literacy had been put in place.

- Pupils were encouraged to read for enjoyment.

How good is our school?

Acknowledgements

Members of the Scottish Library and Information Council Working Group

Marilyn Milligan, Falkirk Council (Chair)
Helen Adair, Moray Council
Rhona Arthur, Scottish Library and Information Council
Caroline Beaton, Perth and Kinross Council
Maggie Gray, Fife Council
Cleo Jones, Edinburgh City Council
Frances Walker, Glasgow City Council

The Working Group would also like to thank all those who contributed to the case studies and assisted with comments and advice.

Sources of Support

Additional information and sources of support can be obtained through the following links:

- *How good is our school?* – self-evaluation using quality indicators
  http://www.hmie.gov.uk

- Scottish Library and Information Council
  http://www.slainte.org.uk